Work in Progress

Becoming a Woman of Honor and Influence

Lisa Gothard

Baptist Publishing House

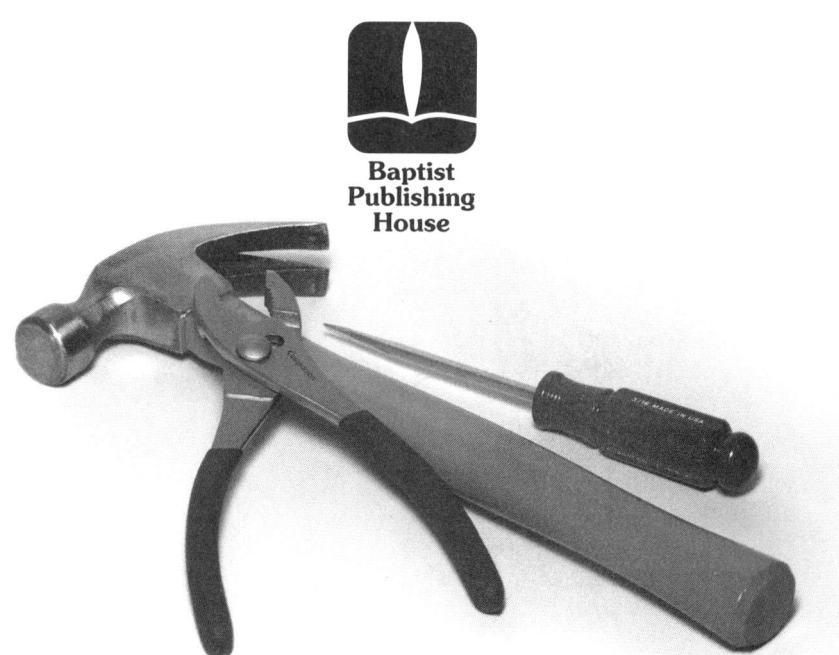

A Work in Progress
Baptist Publishing House
ISBN 0-89114-406-4

All Scripture quotations unless otherwise noted are from the *Holy Bible, King James Version.*

Copyright © 2006 by Baptist Publishing House. All rights reserved. No part of this publication may be reproduced or transmitted in any form or by any means, electronic or mechanical, including photocopy, recording, or any information storage and retrieval system, without permission in writing from the publisher. Requests for permission to make copies of any part of the work should be mailed to: Permissions, Baptist Publishing House, Post Office Box 7270, Texarkana, Texas 75505-7270.

Printed in the United States of America

This book is dedicated first of all to my parents, Foy and Imogene Johnson, who taught me as a young child to follow God and thereby influence others for Him. Thank you both for the godly home and Christian education you supplied me. Second, to my wonderful husband, Paul: you are my encourager and cheerleader. I love being your wife! Thank you for believing in me as well as what God would have me to do. Third, to my children, Michael, Hannah, and Jonathan: may the Lord bless each of you as you grow into the adult He would have you to be. Each of you inspires me to be the best mom I can be. Last, to all my family and friends who have prayed for me as I undertook this endeavor of writing a book: thank you. May the Lord bless each and every one of you as you honor Him and influence others.

Contents

1. Seeking First Things First 7
2. The Heart of the Matter 11
3. Knowing Yourself as a Child of the King 19
4. Conform or Transform 25
5. Faith in the Everyday 31
6. A Compelling Passion.. 37
7. Mastering Your Emotions.. 43
8. Producing Fruit 47
9. What Do Words Have to Do With It? 55
10. Honoring God and Influencing Others............................. 61

Foreword

When Lisa asked me to write a foreword for her book, I was overwhelmed. So many godly women and men have influenced her life who are more qualified than me to write a foreword for this book. So I am honored to write this foreword for my lovely wife.

This is the first book she has written, but I don't think it will be the last. She has worked very hard studying and preparing to get this book out for the WMA. Much great insight can be found in her writings. God has been preparing her for this from birth until now.

Lisa was raised in a godly home, the daughter of a deacon and a godly mother. She also went from kindergarten to twelfth grade at a private Baptist school in north Houston and later attended Pensacola Christian College in Pensacola, Florida. She has been a youth director at two BMAA churches and has taught Sunday School, Sunbeams, and GMAs, and all of that was before she married me. Even as a single woman she served the Lord very faithfully. After we were married, well I'll let her share that with you. There is too much to tell.

The title of her book is *A Work in Progress*. I believe that she got her inspiration from me because I'm a work in progress. I believe that's a great title because we are all a work in progress trying to be more like Jesus. This title reminds me of the children's song "He's Still Working on Me." He works daily in our life, and I know this book will help you have a closer relationship with the Lord.

Lisa is already a woman of honor and influence; I see it every day in her life as a godly mother, daughter, and wife. Those who know her personally already know this, and those who don't will know it as well after you read this book.

Thanks again for this great honor, Lisa. I love you!

Paul Gothard

Introduction

First of all, let me express my thanks to you, the reader, for studying this book. I am praying that it will be a tool used alongside your Bible to bring you to the place God would have you to be in your spiritual walk with Him.

It will take time to read and study this book. Please do not simply rush through the pages as though you are reading the latest novel by your favorite author. Take your time to read, and ask the Lord to show you where you need progress in your spiritual life. Each chapter includes a key verse. Try committing it to memory if you have not already done so. At the end of each chapter is a worksheet. Take time to answer the questions and make decisions. Prepare yourself now to do whatever it takes to draw closer to the Lord during the time you spend with Him as you read these pages along with your Bible.

May the Lord richly bless you as you glorify Him in seeking to be a woman of honor and influence to those around you.

In Christian Love,
Lisa Gothard

1

Seeking First Things First

Matthew 6:33: *"But seek ye first the kingdom of God and His righteousness and all these things shall be added unto you."*

Becoming a woman of honor and influence is no easy task to say the least. Instead it is a process requiring the investment of time and energy. This process may have already begun in your life, or it can begin right now as you read this first chapter. That process involves putting first things first. The key scripture above says it very well. You must seek God first in all things, then He will see to it that everything else is added into your life in the proper place. This chapter will explore how you can begin seeking God first in all that you do so that the rest of your life will be fulfilled. This chapter will be the foundation for the remainder of the book.

Why does God want you to seek Him first? Only one reason exists. He wants to be glorified in every part of your life. Everything you do should bring honor and glory to His name. When God is glorified through you, you have a sense of fulfillment in your life. No greater joy exists than to be right in the center of God's will. *"For I know the thoughts that I think toward you, saith the LORD, thoughts of peace, and not of evil, to give you an expected end. Then shall ye call upon me, and ye shall go and pray unto me, and I will hearken unto you. And ye shall seek me, and find me, when ye shall search for me with all your heart"* (Jeremiah 29:11-13).

God knows the plans that He has for you. He wants only the very best for you. He tells you to seek Him, and you will find

A Work in Progress

Him. He does not play hide-and-seek. He wants to have a personal relationship with you, His creation. Therefore, we will explore three areas of that relationship: salvation, the foundation; sanctification, the process; and salutation, the influence you leave behind.

Let's look at the first step. The first thing necessary for God to take His proper place in your life is to trust Jesus Christ as your personal Savior. John 3:3 says you must be born again. Scripture also says that apart from Jesus Christ you can do nothing. You may be reading this and asking why this statement is in this book, a WMA study book. Surely everyone reading this book is born again! Not necessarily. I have seen many people finally trust Christ as Savior after playing the *game* for many years. It is not worth the risk of your soul to play games with your eternal destiny. Don't think you are okay just because you hold a position in your church or WMA. Jesus said you must be born again to enter into His kingdom. He said He was the way, truth, and life (John 14:6).

This truth returns to the basics for most of you, however if just one person will read this and fully trust Christ as Savior then it is worth writing it. No other foundation can be laid for your Christian faith. You must build upon the foundation of your faith in Jesus Christ. You can't build on your name being on the church roll or who you are in this world. Romans 3:23 tells us that we have all sinned and fallen short of the glory of God. Romans 6:23 tells us that the payment for our sin is death, but the gift of God is eternal life through Jesus Christ our Lord. *"For other foundation can no man lay than that is laid, which is Jesus Christ"* (1 Corinthians 3:11).

You must lay the correct foundation in life if you plan on getting the rest of life right. Jesus said that if you would just call on Him, He would save you. So, do you know you are born again? If you are in doubt, get it settled right now. Stop and pray, asking God to forgive you of your sins and come into your life. Yield control to Him starting right now. If you prayed just now and accepted Christ, I would like to know about it. My address can be found in the back of the book. Write me a note and let me know you have accepted Christ.

Seeking First Things First

After you have trusted Christ as your Savior, life begins to bring on new meaning. Things begin to change for the better, and you begin your journey with Christ. This journey is a process of steps that we call sanctification. Sanctification is the process of cleansing that God uses to make a person like Jesus. It is setting yourself apart for sacred purpose. What did I say earlier is our purpose? To glorify God in all that we do. Sometimes we refer to this process as becoming more like Jesus Christ. Each of the chapters to follow will focus on areas that you can work on to become more sanctified whereby you may honor God and influence others.

Salutation is the close of your life. You can determine how your life will close long before the end arrives. Many times an author will know the ending before she knows the beginning or in-between parts. You can develop this view of your life. Your life is an open book. You have the beginning foundation laid. You know you will strive to be all that God wants you to be. You want to hear the Father say to you, "Well done thou good and faithful servant." Much remains, however, to fill in the pages of your life. Make your salutation such as Paul made his. Look at 2 Timothy 4:7. Paul says, *"I have fought a good fight, I have finished my course, I have kept the faith."* I strive to be able to say that same thing one day. How about you?

Take time right now to set your priorities and make Christ first in all things. Lay the right foundation in your life, then as you build upon that foundation the attacks of Satan cannot topple your life. Hold fast to the sure foundation of Jesus Christ. He is your rock and your hiding place. Set a goal in your life to become more like Jesus. At the end of life you will be rejoicing in what the Lord accomplished through you.

A Work in Progress

Chapter 1

Q & A

for Thought

Here are three ways I can put Jesus first in my life.

1.

2.

3.

Name five things in my life that need to be sanctified.

1.

2.

3.

4.

5.

What kind of influence am I leaving behind for others to follow?

2

The Heart of the Matter

Proverbs 4:23: *"Keep thy heart with all diligence; for out of it are the issues of life."*

Throughout time women, as well as men, have dealt with a plethora of problems. Many have turned to the world for a quick-fix answer to their problems, but eventually realize that drugs, alcohol, sex, or wealth never solve anything. Some have turned to the Bible for answers to those problems and have found the answers that they so desperately needed. With those answers came the cold, hard realization that the seeker had not kept her heart. At some point she dropped her guard and trouble invaded.

Trouble comes in many forms to each of us, usually through the choices that we make. Choices can make us or break us. Joshua told the Israelites to choose whom they would serve, but as for his house they were going to serve the Lord (Joshua 24:15). Joshua made a specific decision for his entire family. He didn't say, "Well, I'm going to serve the Lord. You will have to ask my wife and kids what they are going to do." We need more family leaders to stand and say, *"As for me and my house, we will serve the LORD."* You must set an example to show family the correct choices. Remember, mothers, you have great influence over your family.

Troubles may not mean that you have dropped your guard. They may be a test of your faith. Faith tests are very scary because you don't know at first if you have done something wrong. The Bible tells us in Matthew 5:45 that the rain falls on

A Work in Progress

the just and the unjust. Prayer is necessary at this point. Look over your life to see if you have committed sin. If you do not find sin, then it is probably a faith test. *"There hath no temptation taken you but such as is common to man: but God is faithful, who will not suffer you to be tempted above that ye are able; but will with the temptation also make a way to escape, that ye may be able to bear it"* (1 Corinthians 10:13). In this scripture *tempt* is the same as *test*. Just remember that God is faithful. He will not put more on you than you can bear. Remember also that He knows better than you how much you can bear! After you have checked your guard, then look to Christ as your way of escape.

Whenever you find sin present in your life, it is pretty safe to say that you have not kept your heart as you should have. Let's look at what it means to keep your heart. The word *keep* can also be translated *guard*. Guarding your heart requires attention to what is going on around you. Just as guards are posted at the borders of our nation to keep out those who try to invade or do harm to us, you must post guards on your life to keep out the unwanted elements of sin. You must keep up your guard because that determines what kind of life you will live. Keeping your guard up will allow you to live an abundant life as Christ would have you to live. However, dropping that guard puts you at risk to commit sin. See John 10:10.

Satan wants to destroy your life. If he can accomplish his goal, then he prohibits you from being used by God. He cunningly hides his traps very well. *"Put on the whole armour of God, that ye may be able to stand against the wiles of the devil"* (Ephesians 6:11). It is possible to get caught in his traps before you know what has happened. *Wiles* can be translated as *cunning devices*. Satan and his demons look for ways they can trip you up. They are looking for your weak spots. Remember David? One of his weak spots was women. By his cunning devices Satan used David's weakness to bring about his sin with Bathsheba. Remember Eve? Satan was ever so cunning with her. He twisted what God had said and put doubt in her mind. He likes to use this device quite often. Watch and keep up your guard. Beware!

So, what does the Bible mean by keeping your heart? The

The Heart of the Matter

heart spoken of here is the seat of your emotions, your inner being or will. This inner self must be kept in check for you to be the person God intends you to be. God has a great plan for you and desires that you follow that plan. However, He will not force you to follow His plan. It is up to you to decide to do God's will. Here are some steps you can take to guard your heart.

Be Prepared

Keeping or guarding the seat of your emotions is not the easiest thing to do. You must seek godly wisdom from the Bible as well as godly counselors. You must prepare to do right or you will do wrong. *"He did evil, because he prepared not his heart to seek the LORD"* (2 Chronicles 12:14). Preparation is nine tenths of guarding. You must prepare for anything you set out to do. If you plan a vacation, you must prepare. If you want to be a nurse, doctor, secretary, lawyer, or cashier, you must prepare. If you play sports, you must prepare your body for the task. If you are to survive the storms of life, then you must prepare.

All those who lived in Florida when Hurricane Charley was quickly approaching know now how to be prepared for a storm. Just as you prepare for the physical storms by gathering tools, supplies, food, and water you must prepare for the spiritual storms by seeking God's wisdom and understanding throughout your life. You need your spiritual food, which is the Word of God. You need some spiritual water, which is the Holy Spirit's guidance. You need the Light Who is Jesus, and you need batteries, which is prayer. There truly is power in prayer!

I remember preparing for Hurricane Charley to hit southwest Florida in August 2004. We prepared our home and our family the best that we could. We installed our hurricane shutters on the windows of our home. We bought plenty of water, food, batteries, flashlights, and candles. Then it was time to wait and see where this hurricane would go. One thing I learned is that you cannot wait until the storm is upon you to prepare. You must prepare early. Hurricane Charley was fore-

A Work in Progress

cast to hit Tampa, Florida, 120 miles north of our home in Cape Coral, Florida. Still we prepared. When Hurricane Charley finally made landfall it was only fifteen miles north of our home! We lost our electricity for several days. Many around us lost possessions. Many others lost their homes. Still others lost their lives.

The spiritual storms of life are just as powerful as physical storms of life. They are real and rarely forgotten for years to come. It takes time to recuperate. Make sure you prepare. Prepare your life by hiding God's Word in your heart. His Word is food for the soul. Have a daily time with God. Allowing the Holy Spirit to guide your life is another way to prepare to keep your heart. Be sensitive to the prompts of the Holy Spirit. Prayer connects you to your power source. So pray, pray, pray. Then, Jesus is your shining light. Look to Him for your shelter.

Seek Wisdom

Preparation is also practicing wisdom. Are you seeking godly wisdom? Wisdom is the ability to apply God's knowledge, which enables you to fulfill God's will for your life. You will find God's knowledge through the study of the Bible. It is so important for you to have a daily Bible study and prayer time. You will learn Who He is and how He operates. There is no better way to know God than reading what He has to say and listening to Him during your prayer time.

Proverbs is a great place to start obtaining more wisdom. Look at Proverbs 1:23, *"Turn you at my reproof: behold, I will pour out my spirit unto you, I will make known my words unto you."* Wisdom is speaking here and saying that if you will listen to her correction (reproof) then she will increase your knowledge. A similar promise is found in Psalm 25:14, *"The secret of the LORD is with them that fear him; and he will shew them his covenant."* Wouldn't you rather have the wisdom of God than the wisdom of the world? The wisdom of God can bring health to your body. It can show you the right spouse, career, business and life decisions. Godly wisdom will bring you true and lasting happiness. *"Happy is the man* (or woman) *that findeth wis-*

dom, and the man that getteth understanding" (Proverbs 3:13). *"Wisdom is the principal thing; therefore get wisdom: and with all thy getting get understanding. Exalt her, and she shall promote thee: she shall bring thee to honour, when thou dost embrace her"* (Proverbs 4:7-8).

Wisdom is not something to be taken lightly. You can't just wake up one morning and say, "Okay, I'm gonna be wise today!" Wisdom is a growing process. It is a preparation of your life. Wisdom is knowing how to put to use the knowledge that God has given you. In order to keep your heart you must choose to seek after godly wisdom. Proverbs 9:10 tells us, *"The fear of the LORD is the beginning of wisdom: and the knowledge of the holy is understanding."* Also Proverbs 8:13 states, *"The fear of the LORD is to hate evil: pride, and arrogancy, and the evil way, and the froward mouth, do I hate."* Wisdom begins when you choose to follow Christ and do things His way instead of your own.

Fear the Lord

Since the scriptures above tell us that the fear of the Lord is where wisdom begins, then what is this fear of the Lord? Does it mean that you are scared of God? Does it mean to fear as you would fear a wild animal or snake or natural disaster? No. The fear of the Lord is a reverential fear or respect that you have for God. It knows that God is the very essence of wisdom. It knows that without Him you would surely fail. It knows that you are in the best of care when you follow His direction. It is knowing how undone you are before such a holy One.

Look at Isaiah 6:1-5. *"In the year that king Uzziah died I saw also the Lord sitting upon a throne, high and lifted up, and his train filled the temple. Above it stood the seraphims: each one had six wings; with twain he covered his face, and with twain he covered his feet, and with twain he did fly. And one cried unto another, and said, Holy, holy, holy, is the LORD of hosts: the whole earth is full of his glory. And the posts of the door moved at the voice of him that cried, and the house was filled with smoke. Then said I, Woe is me! for I am undone; because I am a man of unclean lips, and I dwell in the midst of a people of unclean lips: for mine eyes have seen the King, the LORD of hosts."* Isaiah had such an encounter with God that he

A Work in Progress

came away changed. He realized his stature before God and was very humbled in His sight. From this moment on, Isaiah had a different perspective on life. You must come to this point in your walk with Christ. You must catch a glimpse of Who He is so that you can be all He intends for you to be. Catching a glimpse of the holy God enables you to keep or guard your heart.

Respect for God also brings hatred for evil and its relatives, such as pride, lust, and greed. *"Love not the world, neither the things that are in the world. If any man love the world, the love of the Father is not in him"* (1 John 2:15). Here *world* means this world's system and its schemes. Loving the world is the opposite of doing the will of God. Stop for a moment and think where you stand right now. Are you loving the world or doing the will of God? If you find yourself loving the world, which is mostly thinking only of yourself and what makes you happy or feel good, then your guard is down. You can see that you must prepare yourself by turning from the world system or worldly mindset to the mindset of doing the will of God.

Too many people spend their time gaining knowledge of trivial things of this world instead of seeking the wisdom of God. What will matter in a hundred years? Will it matter if you knew the latest scoop on *General Hospital*? Will it matter who won the People's Choice Award for Best Supporting Actress in 2006? Will the world's opinions of the Bible matter? No. Will it matter if you knew Jesus Christ and the forgiveness of your sins? Will it matter how many people you told of Christ and what He could do for them? Will it matter if the life you lived was for worldly pleasure or for heavenly gain? Yes! Stop and ponder these questions. You could add many other questions to the list. What is your position? Are you guarding your heart through preparation? Godly wisdom will improve your attitudes and your lifestyle. Godly wisdom will even lengthen your life (Proverbs 4:9-10).

So choose now to keep your heart with all diligence. Choose now to prepare yourself through godly wisdom. Choose now to follow Christ and what He has for you. Your choices determine your quality of life here on earth as well as in eternity.

The Heart of the Matter

Chapter 2

Q & A
for Thought

What choice or choices have you made in your life to guard your heart?

Name some ways you can prepare yourself spiritually for the battles you will face.

List at least five scripture passages you can memorize to help you guard your heart.

A Work in Progress

3

Knowing Yourself as a Child of the King

First Peter 2:9: *"But ye are a chosen generation, a royal priesthood, an holy nation, a peculiar people; that ye should shew forth the praises of him who hath called you out of darkness into his marvelous light."*

Have you ever asked yourself the question "Who am I?" or "Why am I here?" I am sure at some time or another we have all asked these questions. Some of you have yourself figured out, and some are still working on it. Right? I hope that this chapter will help shed a little light on who you are in Christ and what He intends for you to be.

Knowing yourself is not an easy task. You must identify and confront some things in your life. You can't conquer what you don't confront and you can't confront what you don't identify. You must change the way you see yourself. You are not a product of your past as Satan would have you think. You can overcome your tainted past. Things do not have to be the way they have always been. You can put a stop to the vicious cycle of low self-esteem and worthlessness that has plagued you, but you must take time out to identify these problems and move toward correcting them.

I have a friend who has overcome horrific ordeals in her life and is now a wonderful servant of the Lord. She overcame an abusive childhood. She overcame vicious words against her. Everyone had given up on this girl; even the psychiatrists had given up! But Jesus never gave up. She first heard of Jesus at age eighteen. She accepted Him into her life and has never been the same. Yes, she has struggled. Yes, she went through trials and tests. God allowed those things in her life to make her better for Him. She had training time in the wilderness of her life. Now she is a great pastor's wife and conference speaker whom God is using to change lives everywhere.

God can and wants to do the same for you. All you have to do is let go of the past. Let God change you from the inside out. Start believing what God tells you about yourself. Don't listen to Satan's lies anymore.

You can't overcome your condition until you understand your position. Understanding your position in Christ is vitally important for reaching your God-called destiny. You can do what God has called you to do. *"I can do all things through Christ which strengtheneth me"* (Philippians 4:13).

Let's take a moment and look at the life of Moses beginning in Exodus 4. Moses had been confronted by God at the burning bush in the wilderness while tending sheep. God told Moses what He wanted him to do. Moses began making excuses. Isn't that exactly what we do? Moses gave all his reasons why he could not do what God called him to do. Look at Exodus 4:2. *"And the LORD said unto him, What is that in thine hand?"* Moses had something he could use. To him it was just a rod until God took control. What do you have in your hand? It may seem trivial or menial to you, but when God takes over it becomes a powerful tool. You already possess everything you need to serve God. He has equipped you with it. It may not be polished just yet, but you possess it. Polishing comes over time through various trials in the wilderness. *"Thou hast caused men to ride over our heads; we went through fire and through water: but thou broughtest us out into a wealthy place"* (Psalm 66:12). This psalmist went through some hard times, but was rewarded in the end. You can be like that. You just need to know who you are in Christ. Let's take a look.

"But ye are a chosen generation, a royal priesthood, an holy nation, a peculiar people; that ye should shew forth the praises of him who hath called you out of darkness into his marvelous light"

Knowing Yourself as a Child of the King

(1 Peter 2:9). This verse tells you who you are and why you are here. You are part of a chosen generation. You are part of a royal priesthood. You are part of a holy nation, and, yes, you are a peculiar people. You are a child of the King of kings and Lord of lords. You were born into royalty the moment you accepted Jesus Christ as your personal Savior. Don't you think it is time that you started living like royalty? I am not talking about having a lot of worldly wealth as those of earthly royalty. I am speaking of a lifestyle that exemplifies being a child of God. In other words, you should look like, act like, and speak like a Christian.

My mother and I look a lot alike. Many people throughout the years have recognized me because I look like my mother. I have heard, "You must be Imogene's daughter," too many times to count. My appearance, however, identifies me as her daughter. She cannot deny me no matter how much she may want to at times! I even find myself acting like her and thinking, "Oh, my, I am turning into my mother." Most people cannot tell our voices apart. We have even fooled my husband over the telephone.

A child of God should look like Him, act like Him, talk like Him. I believe you can be more like Him by knowing who you are in Him. First, you must make sure you are in Him. You must first make the choice to accept Jesus Christ as your Savior. You must choose to be born into God's family. It never hurts to review and make sure you are born again. Sin is anything that you think, say, or do that does not please God. The Bible says we have all sinned. *"For all have sinned and come short of the glory of God"* (Romans 3:23). But God has made a way for us to come to Him. *"Jesus saith unto him, I am the way, the truth, and the life: no man cometh unto the Father, but by me"* (John 14:6). *"But as many as received him, to them gave he power to become the sons of God, even to them that believe on his name"* (John 1:12). You must receive Jesus Christ into your life in order to be God's child and live with Him throughout eternity. Take a moment right now to either commit or recommit your life to Christ. If you have never trusted Jesus Christ as your Savior, now is the time to do just that. It only takes a moment to ask Him to forgive you of your sin and come into your life. If you have already asked Christ into your life but you have strayed away from Him, you need to recommit your life to Him right now. Ask Him to forgive you for going astray. Ask Him to restore the joy of your salvation. He will gladly do it if you will only ask.

At the moment you invite Jesus to come into your life something amazing happens. You are born into the family of God. Now I want to make something perfectly clear to you. Once you are born into God's family, you can never be unborn. You can never stop being God's child. Just as I can never stop being my mother's daughter, you cannot stop being God's daughter. Once a baby is born into this physical world can he or she ever be unborn? No. Once you are born into the spiritual world of God's family you can never be unborn.

Not only are you born into God's family, but you are also adopted into His family. *"For as many as are led by the Spirit of God, they are the sons of God. For ye have not received the spirit of bondage again to fear; but ye have received the Spirit of adoption, whereby we cry, Abba, Father. The Spirit itself beareth witness with our spirit, that we are the children of God"* (Romans 8:14-16). Why is it that God has taken so many steps to make you His child? You have been born into His family, and you have also been adopted into His family. Did you know that a child that has been born into a family can be disowned, whereas a child that has been adopted can never be disowned? God is giving you security in knowing that you are His child forever. Adoption is a big thing. Adoption gives you full rights to the riches of the Father. You have been adopted as a full-grown child able to claim your inheritance immediately. There is no waiting period. You have inherited all that is Jesus Christ's. You are a joint heir with Jesus. Doesn't that excite you?

From the passage of Romans 8:14-16 you can see that you can have assurance of your adoption. In verse 16 it says that the Spirit bears witness. In verse 14 it says you are led by the Spirit. In verse 15 it says you can cry *"Abba, Father"* meaning "Daddy God." This is great assurance to you to know that you are God's.

Knowing Yourself as a Child of the King

Many blessings come with being adopted of God. First, you receive a new nature. *"Therefore if any man be in Christ, he is a new creature: old things are passed away; behold, all things are become new"* (2 Corinthians 5:17). Old things are constantly passing away, and all things are constantly becoming new.

Second, you get a new name. *"Him that overcometh will I make a pillar in the temple of my God, and he shall go no more out: and I will write upon him the name of my God, and the name of the city of my God, which is new Jerusalem, which cometh down out of heaven from my God: and I will write upon him my new name"* (Revelations 3:12). The one who overcomes is the one who has Christ as Savior. Jesus says He will make you a pillar in the temple of His God. A pillar is a permanent fixture in a building. It is something that cannot be removed without destroying the building. Therefore, you become a permanent fixture in the heavenly city of New Jerusalem. Jesus will also give you a new name.

Third, you obtain access to God. *"For through him we both have access by one Spirit unto the Father"* (Ephesians 2:18). *"Let us therefore come boldly unto the throne of grace, that we may obtain mercy, and find grace to help in time of need"* (Hebrews 4:16). As God's child you may approach Him with boldness just as your child may approach you and speak with you.

Fourth, you have a fatherly love. *"Behold, what manner of love the Father hath bestowed upon us, that we should be called the sons of God"* (1 John 3:1).

Fifth, you have help in prayer. Matthew 6:5-15 gives you the model prayer and keys to praying to the Father.

Sixth, you receive a spiritual unity. *"Now I am no more in the world, but these are in the world, and I come to thee. Holy Father, keep through thine own name those whom thou hast given me, that they may be one, as we are. That they all may be one; as thou, Father, art in me, and I in thee, that they also may be one in us: that the world may believe that thou hast sent me"* (John 17:11, 21). Jesus prayed this prayer before His crucifixion. He prayed for you and all who would accept Him as Savior to live in unity.

Seventh, you have a glorious inheritance. *"Let not your heart be troubled: ye believe in God, believe also in me. In my Father's house are many mansions: if it were not so, I would have told you. I go to prepare a place for you. And if I go and prepare a place for you, I will come again, and receive you unto myself; that where I am, there ye may be also"* (John 14:1-3). *"And if children, then heirs; heirs of God, and joint-heirs with Christ; if so be that we suffer with him, that we may be also glorified together. For I reckon that the sufferings of this present time are not worthy to be compared with the glory which shall be revealed in us"* (Romans 8:17-18).

You possess all of these awesome assurances as a child of God. These promises help you affirm who you are and what you will be for Christ. Knowing these things gives you a hope above all others. Take these things to heart and apply them where needed in your relationship with the Father. My prayer is that you will know who you are and where you stand with Him so that you can be all that He wants you to be.

Chapter 3

Q & A

for Thought

Why do you think Satan would want you to feel worthless and carry low self esteem around with you? What will he accomplish?

Write a brief description of how you see yourself after reading and studying who you are in Christ.

How does Philippians 4:13 help you in your life?

4

Conform or Transform?

Romans 12:1-2: *"I beseech you therefore, brethren, by the mercies of God, that ye present your bodies a living sacrifice, holy, acceptable unto God, which is your reasonable service. And be not conformed to this world: but be ye transformed by the renewing of your mind, that ye may prove what is that good, and acceptable, and perfect, will of God."*

When you think of the words *conform* and *transform*, which one would you say describes you? Do you conform to your surroundings as a chameleon that changes colors to match its environment? For the chameleon conforming to its environment is a safety mechanism that has been built into its physiological structure to protect it from other animals who would seek to devour and destroy it. Does this sound like you? Do you seek safety in conforming to those with whom you associate?

Linda was a young lady who was just like the chameleon. She conformed to whatever her surroundings happened to be. Linda had attended church as a young girl and had accepted Christ as her Savior. However, she dropped out of church after a short time and never received the discipleship that was so vitally needed in her life. She grew up in the suburban area of Detroit, Michigan, where she encountered a diversity of drugs, alcohol, and gang activity. Linda was soon trapped in a world of conformity that was eating her alive. With both of her parents working long hours at the car assembly plants, she had little to no supervision at home.

She spent most of her time outside of school roaming the

A Work in Progress

streets of Detroit. She joined a gang known as the "Head Bangers." It was in this gang that she was introduced to drugs, alcohol, and immorality. At first she resisted these things, but she wanted to fit in. She wanted to conform. The more she hung out with the gang the more comfortable and conformable she became.

One day at the age of twenty-one an acquaintance invited her to a woman's retreat at a nearby church. Linda decided at the last minute that she would go and check it out. It was there in that service that she began to remember how she had accepted Jesus into her life some ten years before. She began to remember how going to church and Sunday School made her feel happy and free. It was at that moment that she heard these words from the speaker, "Are you conforming or transforming your life?"

We will go back to Linda's story in a moment. Right now I would like for you to ask yourself that question. Are you conforming or transforming your life? Turn to Romans 12:1-2 and let's look at these scriptures together. *"I beseech you therefore, brethren, by the mercies of God, that ye present your bodies a living sacrifice, holy, acceptable unto God, which is your reasonable service. And be not conformed to this world: but be ye transformed by the renewing of your mind, that ye may prove what is that good, and acceptable, and perfect, will of God."*

What I want to do is simply break down this passage of scripture and share from my heart what God has given me for you. Please read on and keep an open mind and heart so the Spirit of God can speak to you through His Word and this book. At times even seasoned Christians tend to conform instead of transform.

Paul wrote his letter to all believers through the Christians at Rome. He began by begging and admonishing them to present themselves to God as a living sacrifice. Why? Because of the mercies of God. Think about how merciful God is to you, not how merciful He is to your spouse, your children, neighbor, the drunk on the street, or anyone else. Really think about how merciful He is to *you*. Let me define *mercy* for you. *Mercy* is "compassion, love, forgiveness, giving or receiving care when it isn't deserved." It is unmerited favor with God. Mercy may withhold or ease expected punishment. Wow! When you look at it with those definitions you can see just how merciful God is to you.

Lamentations 3:22-23 tells us that His mercies are new every morning. We have a fresh supply of God's mercy on hand for us every day. Now that fresh supply does not give you a license to go out and live as your fleshly desires would have you to live. With this mercy comes responsibility. Because we have the mercy of God we are to reciprocate and give ourselves to Him as a living sacrifice. Did you know that it takes more sacrifice to live for Christ than to die for Him? Many of us spend too much time wondering, if it came down to it, would we die for the cause of Christ instead of living for Him now. Living the committed Christian life is a sacrifice. However, it is a sacrifice worth the cost. Since Christ has done so much for us, then it is reasonable for Him to ask that we live holy and acceptable lives. It is the least we can do. It is the expectation that goes along with being a child of God. We are commanded in 1 Peter 1:16 to be *holy* because He is holy.

Conformity is a questionable thing. What does it mean to conform? In Romans 12:2 *conform* means "to adapt to a mode of conduct, to act in accordance with prevailing standards or customs." With this definition in mind we can certainly see how most of us conform to our surroundings. It is easier to go along with the crowd than to stand up for what you believe. The Bible tells us we need to take a stand against conformity. Don't do it! Instead of conformity God wants a transformation to take place in your life.

The renewal of your mind through Bible study and prayer brings about a transformation into the image of His Son. The Father desires this transformation. The transformation that takes place in a caterpillar is amazing. Think about it for a moment. The caterpillar crawls around in the dirt. It doesn't see much other than its immediate surroundings. It eats various types of foliage and plants. Then it goes into the pupal stage. It is covered by its cocoon as a transformation takes place. When it emerges it is no longer the same little creature crawling around on the ground. It has transformed into a beautiful butterfly that can fly high above the ground and see so much more than it could see before. It now feeds on the nectar of beautiful flowers. It is no longer in the trenches of the world where it is stepped on and crushed. It now floats through the air with beauty and ease!

This change pictures the transformation that takes place in a person's life upon accepting Christ as Savior. Before a person comes to Christ she is in the trenches of this world. After coming to Christ there is a metamorphosis which occurs instantly, and she is not the same creature she used to be (1 Corinthians 5:17). The old lifestyle has passed away, and all things have become new. Transformation continues the renewing of the mind through spending time with the Lord. Are you continuing to be transformed into the image of Christ? The process should never stop. It continues until we reach heaven.

Linda listened to all the speaker had to say that night. She was so moved by what was being said that as soon as an altar call was given she left her seat and went forward for counseling. That night Linda renewed her commitment to the Lord and began her life of transformation once again. Do you need to do the same as Linda? Do you need to renew your commitment to the Lord right now? You don't need to wait until you get to church. Stop right now and ask the Lord to renew your spirit. Begin your life of transformation once again. Don't conform any longer to this world and its lies. Go with God and be transformed into the image of Christ. It is not an easy path; however, it is the best path. It is well worth the effort.

Conform or Transform?

Chapter 4

Q & A

for Thought

Name some ways we can conform to the world's standards without realizing it.

What are some actions you can take to allow God to transform yourself into the person He wants you to be?

A Work in Progress

5

Faith in the Everyday

Hebrews 11:6: *"But without faith it is impossible to please him: for he that cometh to God must believe that he is, and that he is a rewarder of them that diligently seek him."*

This verse is used so often that we have become too accustomed to it and pass right over what the Lord wants us to learn from the entire chapter of Hebrews 11. Take time right now to stop and read the entire chapter.

Isn't that a great chapter? These people were ordinary men, women, boys, and girls, just as we are. What was different about them? I believe it was their mindset. They were determined to be winners and not whiners. They chose faith over fear. Here is a verse for you to memorize that deals with fear. *"For God hath not given us the spirit of fear; but of power, and of love, and of a sound mind"* (2 Timothy 1:7).

It is not God Who causes us to fear, so who is it? Satan loves to make us fear. How often does Satan cause you to fear? He does this to me quite often, and many times he succeeds. If he can cause you to fear, your power is diminished, and you will be defeated. God gives you a spirit of power, love, and a sound mind. Satan gives you a spirit of defeat, hatred, and cloudy or unsure mind. So it comes down to whom are you going to believe? Are you going to go with God Who will never fail? Or are you going to listen to Satan as Eve did? Satan simply took what God said and twisted it a little and tricked Eve into believing something that was not true. Has Satan ever done that to you? I am sure he has because he does this with me.

A Work in Progress

Go back once again and read our key verse. The scripture tells us that it is *impossible* to please (or walk with) God without having faith. So not having faith is a *sin*. Wow! Wait a minute, are you sure? Here is something that I have taught to children as well as adults to help them remember what sin is. *Sin is anything that you think, say, or do that does not please God.* So once again, is not having faith sin? Yes!

Now that we have that cleared up, if we are to have faith in order to please God, what is faith? *"Now faith is the substance of things hoped for, the evidence of things not seen"* (Hebrews 11:1). Faith is our hope in Christ. It is believing as if you have seen it with your own eyes. It is a trust in your Lord. It is assurance as if it had already happened. Faith proves to the mind what the physical eye cannot see. Think about this with me for a moment. You have placed your faith in Jesus Christ to secure your eternal destination. Why, then, can you not use that same faith in Jesus Christ to meet your everyday needs? Remember He has told us that He came to give us abundant life (John 10:10). He is not just talking about life in heaven, but the here and now. God wants His children to live life to the fullest in Him. You can only accomplish that goal by having faith in Him to meet your every need. Remember how God dealt with the Israelites as they wandered in the wilderness for forty years. He provided for them on a daily basis. They were not to take more manna than they needed for each day. Their experience teaches me that God's grace is sufficient for today and that His mercies are new every morning.

Look back once again at Hebrews 11. Let's pick out a couple of these ordinary people whom God chose to put in His hall of faith. Look at their lives. Compare them to yourself. How can you have faith as these did? God may not ask you to do some of the things He asked of these folks, however, He might. You better be ready.

First let's look at Abel in verse 4. Abel offered a more excellent sacrifice to God than Cain did. What was it that made his sacrifice more excellent? Was it the quality or quantity of the sacrifice? The story is found in Genesis 4:1-15. Cain and Abel both made offerings unto the Lord from the first fruits of their labors. Cain brought from the fruit of the ground, and Abel brought the first of his flock. They both brought the first fruits as required, so what was the problem? The problem was the attitude behind the offering. God told Cain in verse 7 that he had not done well because sin was at the door of his heart. Many people interpret this verse differently, however, I am going to go with the thinking that Cain had a bad attitude. He did not give his offering by faith. Maybe he didn't want to give the best he had in fear that he wouldn't have anything good left for himself. Abel, however, gave the best he had in faith. Abel trusted that God would provide what he needed.

Do you have the faith that God is going to provide what you need? That's a lot easier said than done. Think of a time when God asked you to give an offering. Maybe it was your last bit of money, and you weren't getting paid for a week. Did you do it? Or did you say, "God, I can't do that." Remember, God will never ask you to do something that He cannot take care of. He will always see you through.

Second, look at the example of Noah in Hebrews 11:7. Pretend you are Noah. God has just come to you and told you His plan to flood the earth, and that you must build an ark. How would you react? I would have a lot of questions. What is rain? It's never done that before. God, I know nothing about building a big boat. I'm scared of lions, tigers, and bears. You want me to put two of every creature on this boat with me? Help! It surely took a huge act of faith. Noah worked on this boat for 120 years. Only his family believed with him what God had said. Noah's action was a great testimony of his home life. He did not sit around at home and complain about what God had told him to do. He acted in faith and led his family in the right direction. What has God asked you to do? Are you doing it? Are you by faith leading your family in the right direction, or are you complaining and whining about what God has asked you to do? He is not asking you to build a big boat and fill it with two of every animal. He may just be asking you to tell your friend or family member about His saving grace. He may be asking you to step out in faith and teach that Sunday School class, WMA class, or auxiliary class. Whatever it is, step out in

A Work in Progress

faith. He will help you through it.

I remember when Paul and I were first married, I moved my membership to his home church. I attended the WMA meetings on Sunday nights. The president kept saying, "Ladies, we need a teacher for this year. Who is going to be our teacher? We really need to pray about this." I remember feeling the prompting of the Holy Spirit that I was to be the teacher. I said, "Lord, I can't do that. My mother-in-law is in the class; I have sisters-in-law in here. The pastor's wife is in here; my Sunday School teacher is in here. I'm the youngest person in the room. Many other ladies are much more qualified than I am." Still, God said I was to do this. Finally, a couple of weeks later I told them that I would like to teach the class. I learned more by teaching that class than if I had been sitting there listening to someone else. I survived just fine. Don't ever think you can't do something God has asked you to do. He is the enabler. He just wants a vessel to work through.

Many other examples of faith can be found in Hebrews 11. I will leave that to your own study. I do want you to think about this though. The hall of faith is not complete yet. What are you writing for your verse? By faith, Lisa…; by faith, Tammy…; by faith, Sue…. What are you doing that requires you to step out in faith? Or are you holding back because of fear that Satan has placed in your heart? A life of faith is a life of joy. A life of faith is one of adventure. A life of faith is worth it all because it pleases God. Are you living your life by faith? You can start today.

Faith in the Everyday

Chapter 5

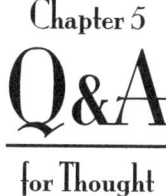

Q&A
for Thought

What is it that God would have you to do by faith?

What hinders you from living a life of faith? How can you overcome those obstacles?

A Work in Progress

6

A Compelling Passion

Matthew 6:21: *"For where your treasure is, there will your heart be also."*

All of us are passionate about something. Some are passionate about education, others about nature, others about human rights, still others about animal rights or sports. Nothing is wrong with any of these passions; however, sometimes as Christians, I think passion is misplaced.

What exactly is a passion? *Passion* is "an intense, driving, or overmastering feeling or conviction; a strong liking, desire for, or devotion to some activity, object, or concept." One may also use the words *enthusiasm,* or *zeal* which means "intense emotion-compelling action, devotion to a cause." Passion, when referring to the passion of Christ, refers to suffering. These definitions reveal that passion is an extremely powerful emotion or driving force.

So let me ask once again, what is your passion? Do you even have a passion? Almost every person has a passion about someone or something. As a Christian, a follower of Jesus Christ, it is safe to say that He should be your number one passion. Matthew 6:21 tells us *"For where your treasure is, there will your heart be also."* You will be passionate about whatever it is that you treasure the most.

Your highest and most important treasure should be Jesus Christ and what He has done in your life. Sadly, there are very few who seem to truly care about what Christ has done for them. You may be one of those who says you care. You have accepted Him as your Savior. You may even keep the Ten Commandments as best you can. But when it comes down to it, are you passionate about Jesus? Do you tell those with whom you come in contact about His saving, life-changing power? You have something to shout from the rooftop of the Sears Tower in Chicago or from the rooftop of your own home. You have been pardoned from a debt that you could not pay. That should be enough to make any born-again believer shout hallelujah for the entire world to hear, right?

A revisit to the day you accepted Christ into your life might just stir up that passion once again. Take just a moment with me if you will and revisit that time when you consciously made the decision to turn your life over to Christ. Do you remember the relief you felt inside? Do you remember the joy and excitement? Maybe you are a less emotional person and didn't feel anything at the point of salvation. That's okay. I am sure, though, at some point not long after your salvation you experienced a sense of joy and calmness that had not been present before. Go to that place with me for a moment. Think about the joy, calmness, relief, and excitement that you experienced. Does it bring a smile to your face?

You can obtain that passion once again by beginning to share your faith with others. You will be amazed at how enthusiastic you may become about what Jesus has done for you by simply telling others. Begin by telling others about your salvation experience and how they can be saved as well. Then begin to notice everyday ways God chooses to build your faith. Maybe you received a phone call from a friend when you were feeling lonely. Or maybe some unexpected money arrived to help with a financial need. You can share these experiences with others, and it will help keep your passion alive.

You may say your passion is dead. How can you revive it? Take your Bible and turn to John 3:16. Read it out loud. This verse is the gospel in a nutshell. If you can just get this one verse etched into your mind, you will have a passion for the lost around you. Think of it. Every second of every day someone enters into eternity. They either perish or have everlasting life. What are you doing about those with whom you come in

A Compelling Passion

contact? Are you giving your best effort to point them toward everlasting life? Remember, everyone will spend eternity somewhere. It will either be heaven or hell. Take as many to heaven with you as you can. Be passionate about telling others of Christ because in a hundred years that is all that will matter. It won't matter how passionate you were about your hobby or sports or your activist group. It will only matter whom you influenced for Jesus Christ. People really do need the Lord.

Paul, my husband, sings the song "People Need the Lord." He sang this at almost every service during our deputation for North American missions, yet every time I hear that song it still burns deep into my heart and brings tears to my eyes. People really are hurting and dying and spending an eternity without Jesus Christ in a devil's hell. It is time that you begin to do something about it. Yes, you read that correctly. It is time for you to do your part. Get busy telling those God has entrusted to you about His saving grace. Begin with your friends, neighbors, associates, and relatives. Invite them to attend church with you.

If you are not prepared to share the gospel with them, study and become prepared. The Roman road is an easy presentation. Mark your Bible beginning with John 3:16. Beside John 3:16 write Romans 3:23. Beside Romans 3:23 write Romans 5:8. Beside Romans 5:8 write Romans 6:23, and then beside Romans 6:23 write Romans 10:9, 10, 13. Lead someone through these scriptures and explain in your own way what they mean to you and how Christ has changed your life. God wants to use you to lead others to Him. Let Him use you. Become passionate about souls. It brings eternal rewards like nothing else on earth. It is time that you get out of your comfort zone and tell someone who is lost and going to hell about the saving power of Jesus Christ before it is too late.

I would like to share with you the story of Marina. Marina has touched my life in a very special way, and I will never be the same since coming to know her. In February 2002 I first knocked on her door. Paul and I were out in a neighborhood in North Fort Myers, Florida, inviting people to come and worship with us at a new church in their area. She answered her door almost with disgust. She had just returned from the emergency room because of an illness with her pregnancy of five months. She had no interest in who we were or what we wanted to share with her; however, she said that her eight-year-old son, Cedrick, could go with us to church. She allowed us to pray with her about her pregnancy, and we went on our way.

Cedrick began attending every Sunday. He would go home after every service and tell his mom what he had learned at church and how he wanted her to come with him. Not a Saturday went by that we did not go by her home and check on her and make sure Cedrick would be coming to church the next day. Most of those Saturdays she avoided us and would have Cedrick talk with us. We kept praying and pursuing. Finally, on Mother's Day 2002, she promised Cedrick she would come to church with him. She had lost her job the week before and had nothing else to do. This was definitely a God appointment.

Paul preached a message on being a godly mother. At the end of the service Marina walked the aisle and said she needed Jesus in her life. I had the privilege of opening my Bible and showing her how to trust Jesus as her Savior. After reading the scriptures and answering her questions, she was ready to pray and ask Jesus into her life. After she prayed, she was visibly a different woman from when she walked in the door that morning. Christ's changing power was very evident in her. She no longer wanted to live as she had been living. She had a very rough past. She had moved to the United States from Colombia at the age of fifteen in 1990. She had gotten involved with the wrong crowd and influences in her life. She was very similar to the woman at the well in John 4. She immediately changed, however, when she met Jesus.

It was my privilege to help Marina through many of life's circumstances and teach her the godly way she should handle things. She became part of our family while we were in Florida. She refers to me as her mom, and I am proud to call her my daughter. She has come a long way in her walk with the Lord and continues to grow in Him. Now she has a passion for others and wants to share Jesus with them.

A Compelling Passion
Chapter 6
Q & A
for Thought

Where is my passion? Is it on temporal or eternal things?

If I were to encounter someone today who needed Christ in her life, would I be able to show her how to trust Jesus as her Savior?

List the verses you would use to lead someone to Christ.

Who am I discipling right now to have a passion for others?

A Work in Progress

7

Mastering Your Emotions

Ephesians 5:15: *"See then that ye walk circumspectly, not as fools, but as wise."*

Did you know that you don't always have to be right? You don't always have to have it your way, nor do you always have to be first. I realize this is probably a shock for some of you, right? Most wives and mothers have learned these lessons; however, sometimes you don't practice these truths in all of your life circumstances. Now I am not saying that you should never be first or have it your way, but many times your demands on others give the impression you are a very proud, self-righteous person. Christ does not want others to see us that way. When others look at us, they are to see Christ in everything, even in our emotions. We are going to study several different aspects of our emotions and apply God's Word to them.

Pride

Have you ever felt it's my way or no way; I'm right, you're wrong; I'm better than you. Maybe you have gone into a store or restaurant and demanded your way by causing a scene, then gotten caught as a church friend came in and said something to you such as, "Hey, there. I just saw you at church. You sure got here quick." The person helping you is totally turned off of church, God, and Jesus.

We have all had similar circumstances take place that we are not very proud of. We must realize that pride is an emotional tactic that Satan uses against us to cause us to sin. He did this with the first woman, Eve, and he does it with each of us today. God tells us, *"Pride goeth before destruction, and an haughty spirit before a fall"* (Proverbs 16:18). Satan wants you to think that pride will build you up, but God says pride brings destruction.

Another matter of pride is thinking that everyone needs to know your opinion on a matter. Our opinions don't matter most of the time. Remember to think before you speak. Ask yourself if you really need to say what you are getting ready to say. Even when you are being persecuted for the sake of Christ, be careful of what you say. Remember all the beatings Jesus suffered, yet He opened not His mouth. He humbled Himself even when He rightfully could have opened His mouth. Choose wisely when you should speak and when you should keep silent. Satan will be looking for every opportunity to make you proud and puffed up. Jesus wants you to be humble with a kind spirit.

Anger

Anger is the one emotion we all try to justify most of the time. After all, the Bible does talk about righteous indignation! God tells us, *"Be ye angry, and sin not: let not the sun go down upon your wrath"* (Ephesians 4:26). The problem is that nine times out of ten we get angry and sin.

How is it possible to be angry and not sin? Anger must be dealt with immediately. If it is ventilated thoughtlessly, anger will hurt others and destroy relationships. If anger is bottled up inside you, it can cause bitterness and destroy from within. If anger is nursed, Satan is given the opportunity to divide us. Many people will not recognize that Satan is behind the scenes taking every opportunity he can find to destroy family and friends. Please recognize Satan's tactics and don't fall prey to his schemes. Don't let petty things cause you to remain angry. Deal with your anger immediately to keep your relationship with the Lord fresh.

Throughout scripture we are admonished to be like Jesus. *"The LORD is merciful and gracious, slow to anger, and plenteous in*

Mastering Your Emotions

mercy" (Psalm 103:8). Here is an attribute we need to place in our lives to be like Jesus. We need to be *"slow to anger."* A quick temper will get you into trouble. If you have a quick temper, you probably have a quick mouth as well and fly off the handle very easily. Christ would not have you to act like that. It is definitely not honoring to God or a positive influence on others. Learn to hold your tongue. Be slow to anger, and take it to the Lord in prayer. Quit saying you can't help how you feel, and go pray. If you are praying for someone who has angered you, the Lord will calm your spirit and the anger will be dealt with properly. Don't give Satan any more opportunities in your life. Take things immediately to the Lord.

Offended or Hurt Feelings

Ladies, we need to stop letting our feelings run (ruin) our lives. Too often we allow something someone said or did to offend us or hurt our feelings. It is time that we toughen up and recognize another tactic of Satan. Most of the time the person who allegedly hurt your feelings didn't mean to do so, but Satan meant to. Satan is trying to offend you so you can't grow spiritually. If you are whining and pouting about someone hurting your feelings, get over it. Quit being a spiritual baby.

"Then shall many be offended, and shall betray one another, and shall hate one another" (Matthew 24:10). This scripture is talking about what will happen in the end times. This picture shows what is going on today. This end-time attack falls on all believers. Satan wants you to be offended so you will not be useful to the Lord. If you are offended by another, get it right. Go talk with the person and work things out. Life is too short to go around with hurt feelings or offenses. When someone hurts you, the first thing you should do is pray. Tell the Lord about it. Ask Him to help you lay aside a grudge or calm your anger. Ask Him to help you to drop it.

Discouragement

Many times throughout our lives we become discouraged. God does not want us to be discouraged or downhearted. People with negative comments or mockery often try to discourage us. David's brothers and other members of the Israelite army tried to discourage David from fighting Goliath. (See 1 Samuel 17:28-32.) David, however, did not focus on their negative words. He knew that with God on his side he could accomplish anything God would have him to do.

Recognize discouragement when it begins to come into your life. The key to overcoming discouragement is, once again, prayer. Prayer is the key to dealing with all life's difficulties. People all around you are watching you. They are watching to see how you will react to situations. Don't allow Satan to discourage you. He wants to keep you where you are. God wants you to go beyond where you could even imagine. Go with God and beat discouragement. *"Being confident of this very thing, that He which hath begun a good work in you will perform it until the day of Jesus Christ"* (Philippians 1:6). You can be assured that Jesus will see you through any difficulty you may face.

Chapter 7

for Thought

What emotions in my life do I need to keep in check and allow the Holy Spirit to control?

List a scripture for each emotion on your list and commit it to memory.

8

Producing Fruit

Galatians 5:22-23: *"But the fruit of the Spirit is love, joy, peace, longsuffering, gentleness, goodness, faith, meekness, temperance: against such there is no law."*

We have all heard many messages on the fruit of the Spirit. We have read books, listened to tapes, even taught lessons on the subject. Here's my question. Do we really have the evidence of the fruit in our lives? Can someone who does not know you simply observe you in a situation and say there goes a Christian because I can see the evidence of Christ in her?

In Mark 11:11-14 Jesus passed a fig tree on His way from Bethany to Jerusalem. He was hungry, and when He was still a good ways from it, saw that it had leaves. It looked great on the outside from a distance, yet when Jesus got close and wanted its fruit, He found none. Usually when a fig tree had many large leaves, it also had fruit. This tree, however, had none. You might say it was pretty on the outside, but empty on the inside. Therefore, Jesus cursed the tree saying it would never bear fruit.

Christians can become just like that fig tree. We can have all the right answers to religion. We can look the part outwardly. Yet inwardly we are empty. We produce no fruit. Many people mistake such things as how much you know about the Bible for fruit. Scripture tells us otherwise. Jesus said we are to bear much fruit, which only the Holy Spirit can produce in our lives. Let's take a look at these fruits in the life of the Christian.

A Work in Progress

Love

Our first love ought to be a love for God. We should love God naturally. After all, He first loved us and gave Himself for us. *"Jesus said unto him, Thou shalt love the Lord thy God with all thy heart, and with all thy soul, and with all thy mind"* (Matthew 22:37). Jesus declared this commandment to be His greatest. Think on this verse for a moment. Many claim to love Him with all their being, yet they turn around and take His name in vain or blaspheme Him. Many fail to recognize or appreciate His blessings upon their lives. Have you stopped lately and counted your blessings? It will open your eyes and renew your love for the Lord if you will stop and count your blessings.

Don't allow your love for the Lord to cool. *"Unto the angel of the church of Ephesus write; These things saith he that holdeth the seven stars in his right hand, who walketh in the midst of the seven golden candlesticks; I know thy works, and thy labour, and thy patience, and how thou canst not bear them which are evil: and thou hast tried them which say they are apostles, and are not, and hast found them liars: and hast borne, and hast patience, and for my name's sake hast laboured, and hast not fainted. Nevertheless I have somewhat against thee, because thou hast left thy first love. Remember therefore from whence thou art fallen, and repent, and do the first works; or else I will come unto thee quickly, and will remove thy candlestick out of his place, except thou repent"* (Revelations 2:1-5).

Jesus addressed a group of Christians who hated the evil which was present in the world. They spoke against false teachers. They were hard workers in the local church. However, there was a great problem. Ladies, ministry and true doctrine are worthless without devotion to Christ to back it up. Too often we get caught up in what the church is doing. Our focus is on service to our church or auxiliary. We become confused by thinking that our service for the Lord is our relationship. It is not!

Think about your relationship with your husband. Is your relationship based on service? No. It is based on your love for him. The more time you spend with him, the more you love him. So should our relationship be with Jesus Christ. Our

Producing Fruit

number one focus should be Jesus Christ and our relationship with Him. If you find yourself too busy to spend time with the Lord every day, then you are too busy. To have a strong relationship one must work on making it strong by spending time with the other. Jesus is waiting for you to return to your first love – Him.

Not only should your love for God be evident, but also your love for fellow believers. A very unique relationship exists with those who have trusted Christ as Savior. You possess a kinship like no other. When Christians meet for the first time, it seems as though they have known each other forever. That is the Spirit bearing witness. What has happened to love among Christians? *"We know that we have passed from death unto life, because we love the brethren. He that loveth not his brother abideth in death"* (1 John 3:14).

Love for other believers gives evidence of being a Christian. Go back to loving others. Let the past be the past, and return to loving people. Don't worry about what this person or that person did. Remember what you did to Christ, yet He still loves you. God is the One to keep account of what people do. He is the judge. Take time to study 1 Corinthians 13, known as the love chapter. Many good attributes can be applied from these scriptures.

Joy

"These things have I spoken unto you, that my joy might remain in you, and that your joy might be full" (John 15:11).

If you will take a moment and read the verses preceding John 15:11, you will find that Jesus is speaking about bearing fruit and love. Love and joy are linked together. Without love there is no joy. With proper love there is fullness of joy. Your relationship with the Lord produces joy. Your service for the Lord brings joy.

Being joyful in life doesn't always mean things are going great and you are happy-go-lucky. Joy is a deep possession regardless of the circumstances of life. Happiness is only superficial. Happiness changes with your circumstances. Joy never changes with circumstances. Joy is constant because it is the realization that it comes from Christ alone. *"Thou wilt shew me the path of life: in thy presence is fulness of joy; at thy right hand there are pleasures for evermore"* (Psalm 16:11). True joy comes from a close relationship with Jesus Christ. It comes by following His plan for your life. It comes by being in His presence. Focus on Jesus and joy will naturally become a fruit in your life.

Peace

"Let the peace of God rule in your hearts, to the which also ye are called in one body; and be ye thankful" (Colossians 3:15).

Peace with God and the peace of God are two different types of peace. You obtained peace with God when you trusted Jesus Christ as your Lord and Savior. You must constantly work on the peace of God. Having the peace of God requires you to submit to what God wants in your life. Peace comes from knowing and doing His will in everyday life situations. Satan comes and tries his best to steal our peace and keep us in turmoil. Do not allow him to take away your peace. Do not listen to his lies. *"Peace I leave with you, my peace I give unto you: not as the world giveth, give I unto you. Let not your heart be troubled, neither let it be afraid"* (John 14:27). True peace comes from Jesus alone. The world will give false peace which does not last. Jesus' peace will last through eternity.

Longsuffering

Another word we could use here would be *endurance*. Many times we must endure difficult circumstances in our lives. We must hold fast to our faith in Jesus Christ knowing that He will make a way through the rough times. Job was longsuffering. He endured much more than any of us could ever imagine, yet he held fast to his faith in God. Paul also endured many hardships. He admonished Timothy in 2 Timothy 4:5-8 to endure afflictions. Paul had fought a good fight, and he was now ready to meet the Lord. May we also be able to say that at the end of our lives. Endurance builds character into our lives. Take your trials to the Lord in prayer, and leave them with Him. Christ will enable to you endure every challenge.

Producing Fruit

I think of many friends and family who have suffered physical afflictions, yet have endured through the grace of God and have overcome those problems. They did not allow their circumstances to make them bitter, but better. The next time you face a hardship remember those who have gone through similar circumstances before you and have come out stronger in their faith. Be faithful to the Lord, and He will see you through.

Gentleness

Gentleness is mildness combined with tenderness. Being a gentle person does not make you a doormat to be walked upon. Jesus was a very gentle person, yet He did not allow people to walk over Him. Gentleness is actually a great strength. *"Take my yoke upon you, and learn of me; for I am meek and lowly in heart: and ye shall find rest unto your souls"* (Matthew 11:29).

A gentle spirit relieves anxiety. It leads to rest for your soul. All too often I see folks who put aside that gentleness for a rough exterior that says nobody is going to hurt them anymore. That rough exterior and lack of gentleness, mildness, and tenderness causes problems in their relationships with people as well as with God. Ask God to give you a gentle spirit. Work on being kind to others. Allow this fruit of the Spirit to become abundant in your life.

Goodness

"Therefore all things whatsoever ye would that men should do to you, do ye even so to them: for this is the law and the prophets" (Matthew 7:12).

Here it is right in Scripture – the Golden Rule. God has given us a great verse to live by. If you don't want someone doing a certain thing to you, then don't do it to them.

Many times we may hear someone say they did something out of the goodness of their heart. Where does goodness come from? All that is good comes from God. We need to remember we are not good on our own. If left to ourselves, we would choose evil over good. Remember the Golden Rule and Matthew 7:12 the next time you have a question as to how you should act or respond to a situation.

Faith

It seems strange to me that a person can have faith enough to trust Christ as Savior for eternity, but when it comes to faith for everyday needs, she finds it hard to muster up that kind of faith. Ladies, faith is faith. You and I can have the confidence that just as our salvation is secure in Him so He will care for us from day to day. *"Wherefore, if God so clothe the grass of the field, which to day is, and to morrow is cast into the oven, shall he not much more clothe you, O ye of little faith? Therefore take no thought, saying, What shall we eat? or, What shall we drink? or, Wherewithal shall we be clothed? (For after all these things do the Gentiles seek:) for your heavenly Father knoweth that ye have need of all these things"* (Matthew 6:30-32).

Depend on the Lord to take care of your needs on a daily basis. He will never let you down. He will always see you through. When the tough times come, exercise your faith. Faith will remove the distance between you and God. *"Trust in the LORD with all thine heart; and lean not unto thine own understanding. In all thy ways acknowledge him, and he shall direct thy paths"* (Proverbs 3:5-6).

Meekness

Many people have the wrong idea when it comes to this fruit of the Spirit. Some seem to think that meekness is the same as weakness. It is far from that. Meekness is strength under control. Meekness is humility toward God and mildness towards people. Moses is a prime example of meekness. He was a great leader of the people of Israel. According to Numbers 12:3, he was meeker than anyone on the earth. He was a strong and courageous leader of God's people. He was selfless in his thoughts and concerns. He wanted what was best for everyone around Him. What if we as women would take on this attitude of meekness? What would happen in our families, neighborhoods, and churches? I believe we would begin to see a great movement toward God. People would begin to

Producing Fruit

wonder what was going on and why women were being so unselfish and thoughtful. Wouldn't that be a great day? Remember to work on the characteristic of meekness in your life. Allow the Holy Spirit to control you and direct you into a life of meekness.

Temperance

Temperance is better known as self control. We must learn to bring our mind, body, and emotions into control. Many times we find ourselves jumping to conclusions because of a mind that is not in control. We find ourselves lashing out at others because our emotions are not in check. Our bodies are to be brought under subjection. First Corinthians 9:24-27 tells us to run the race of the Christian life in order to attain the prize. In order to attain the prize, one must be in self control. We must set a goal of winning the Christian life. Don't allow Satan to defeat you in this race. You can win. Winning takes courage to face what is ahead and go for the finish line. Don't look back. Stay focused on the prize ahead — heaven.

You know where self control is needed in your life. Even better than self control is the Holy Spirit's control. Turn these areas over to the Holy Spirit, and allow Him to train you and bring those things into control. If you will allow the Spirit to have control, you will win the prize.

A Work in Progress
Chapter 8
Q & A
for Thought

Which fruit of the Spirit is most evident in my life?

Which fruit do I need to work on the most, and how can I improve?

9

What Do Words Have to Do With It?

Psalm 19:14: *"Let the words of my mouth, and the meditation of my heart, be acceptable in thy sight, O LORD, my strength, and my redeemer."*

We could spend much time on many topics about how to be women of honor and influence. However, I don't think of one more important than that of speaking wisely. Although actions do speak louder than words, our words still speak quite loudly. Words carry great power. Just take the three little words *I love you*. These words spoken to certain people become very powerful. They make children feel secure. They make your spouse more confident. They bring tears to a mother's eyes.

We will study two areas in this chapter. First, we will explore the power of words spoken to others. Second, we will explore the power of words spoken to ourselves.

The Power of Words Spoken to Others

Did you know that your words are like windows which give others a glimpse into your heart? Your words express who you are, what you believe, and what you think. Careless words can damage or ruin our relationships. However, by God's grace, damaged relationships can be rebuilt by words which show respect, kindness, compassion, forgiveness, and warmth.

James, the brother of Jesus, had much to say about the tongue and our words. His New Testament book addresses

A Work in Progress

some unethical practices and teaches right Christian living. So let's see what James has to say to us about our speech. *"Wherefore, my beloved brethren, let every man be swift to hear, slow to speak, slow to wrath: for the wrath of man worketh not the righteousness of God. Wherefore lay apart all filthiness and superfluity of naughtiness, and receive with meekness the engrafted word, which is able to save your souls"* (James 1:19-21).

First of all, these verses tell us to *listen* before we speak. Have you ever wondered why God gave us two ears and only one mouth? Maybe we are to listen twice as much as we speak. Sadly most Christians speak twice as much as they listen. The Bible tells us we are to be *slow* to speak. We need to think about what we are getting ready to say. The words we speak will either build someone up or tear them down. What are you speaking? *"Be ye kind one to another, tenderhearted, forgiving one another, even as God for Christ's sake hath forgiven you"* (Ephesians 4:32). If the words you are getting ready to speak are not kind and tenderhearted, then you better rethink your words. Unfortunately many Christians get wound up and ready to fire their hurtful words whenever the opportunity arises.

I'd like to suggest to those of you who are married that you govern your speech to your spouse for just one day and see what happens. Let nothing come out of your mouth that is not kind, tenderhearted, and forgiving. He will recognize a difference, and his attitude will change as well. Watch your body language as well. A lot of time we can say one thing with the mouth, but another with the body.

I would venture to say that most of the words spoken among us today are idle, negative words. *"Let the words of my mouth, and the meditation of my heart, be acceptable in thy sight, O LORD, my strength, and my redeemer"* (Psalm 19:14). You may be reading these words and saying to yourself that there is no way you can keep your mouth closed and not say what you feel. It has to come out. No, it does not. If you are following Christ, then your words are to be acceptable to Him. This scripture tells us that not only our words, but what we think and dwell on are also to be acceptable to Him. How is that possible? It is only possible because He is your strength and your Redeemer.

What Do Words Have to Do With It?

"I can do all things through Christ which strengtheneth me" (Philippians 4:13). You can do anything you really want to do. The problem is that most of the time you don't want to be controlled in that area. You must make a conscious decision to allow the Holy Spirit to have control of your mouth. If you truly want to be a woman of honor and influence, then you must watch what you say and how you say it. I have looked up to many ladies over the years whom I have finally had the opportunity to talk to. Some of them encouraged me, while others disappointed me by what they chose to talk about and how they talked about it. Ladies, let us ever be mindful of what we are saying and how we are saying it.

Allow me to be very straightforward. Pastor's wife, be very careful how you speak of your husband. Remember he is God's man. You are to build him up and not tear him down. Ladies, negativity ought not come out of your mouth about your husband, unless it is to God in your private prayer time. If you have negativity to share, share it with the One Who can do something about it. Don't ruin his reputation or testimony over something that shouldn't be discussed with the girls. The same goes for any other wife. Husband bashing is one of my pet peeves. Remember you two have become one, and you are the one who chose to marry him, so deal with it. Watch what you say and how you say it.

Your choice of words should not be limited to just those between you and your spouse. You need to watch your choice of words in any circumstance. People are always watching and listening. Remember to pray daily for the Lord's guidance in your choice of words.

Who is motivating your speech? Do you find that your speech is full of jealousy, selfishness, unspiritual thoughts and ideas, earthly concerns, disorder, or evil? Then it is safe to say that the motivator of your speech is Satan. However, if your speech is that of mercy, peace, love, courtesy, goodness, and gentleness, then the motivator is God and His wisdom. Let this sink into your soul. Meditate on these things for a few moments and take time to get things right with God.

Let's not beat around the bush any longer. I'm going to come right out and say something that needs to be said. Ladies, the gossip among us must stop. Do not be a part of spreading gossip through the means of the telephone ministry or the prayer chain. The prayer chain is a great ministry tool, however, we must be careful not to misuse it. Many times we say more than needs to be said about someone who needs our prayers. You or I could end up in some of the same situations as those we gossip about if not for the grace of God. I am reminded of the children's song that says, "Oh be careful little mouth what you say."

Let's look at James 3:2-12. James once again addresses an issue in the early church that is very relevant for today. We all have a problem controlling our tongue. We all, at some time or another, have offended someone with our words (verse 2). We seem to be able to control many things; however, our tongue is one of the most difficult (verses 3-5). You know as well as I do that our tongues can get us into a heap of trouble if we allow it. We must learn to control it. Even something said that we feel is insignificant can grow to something out of control (verses 5-6). Use these three little questions before you speak. Is what I want to say true? Is it necessary? Is it kind? If the answer to any of these questions is no, then don't speak. Most of the time we just ask the first question. The answer is yes so we proceed to dismember, discredit, and destroy someone else.

James compares the tongue's damage to that of a raging fire (verse 6). The uncontrolled tongue can do horrible damage. It is one of the devices Satan uses most to pit people against one another. Idle words are damaging because they spread destruction as quickly as wildfire. No one can stop the results once they are spoken. We shouldn't be so careless as to think we can say what we want then apologize later. The words have done their damage, which cannot be reversed no matter how much you apologize. We must learn to let the Holy Spirit have control of our speech. He is the only One Who can give us the power to control the things we say.

The Power of Words Spoken to Self

Not only must we control what we say to others, but we must also control the words we speak to ourselves. We can

What Do Words Have to Do With It?

hurt and paralyze ourselves with negative self-talk. Do you ever find yourself saying, "God can't use me because...," or, "Why would anyone want to be my friend"? Maybe you have said or thought, "I failed, so I will always be a failure."

What we think about ourselves affects us emotionally, physically, and spiritually. We don't have to be helpless victims of our own thought patterns. We can overcome through Jesus Christ. We must transform our minds as we replace lies with the truths of God's Word. How are we transformed? We are transformed by the renewing of our minds (Romans 12:2). You renew your mind with Scripture, not with self-help books, worldly influences, or any other way. Allow the Word to renew your mind. Second Corinthians 5:17 tells us that we are a new creation in Christ Jesus. We are not the same as we used to be. We are continually getting rid of the old things, and all things are becoming new. Take time to read what Ephesians 1 has to say about the children of God. Also read Psalm 139. God can get good out of anything or anyone if you get in agreement with Him.

You must remember that negative speech grieves the Holy Spirit. It makes others think negatively of you. You must believe positive things about yourself. You will never go beyond what you believe about yourself no matter what God has for you. So get in agreement with God and enjoy all that He has for you.

A Work in Progress

Chapter 9

Q & A
for Thought

In what areas do I need to change my speech to be more positive and Christlike?

How have I listened to Satan and allowed myself to speak negatively?

What steps do I need to take in order to speak more like Christ?

10

Honoring God and Influencing Others

First Timothy 1:17: *"Now unto the King eternal, immortal, invisible, the only wise God, be honour and glory for ever and ever. Amen."*

We have covered a lot of ground in this book. From a personal standpoint this has been one of the most difficult tasks I have ever undertaken. I want to thank you for taking time to read and study this book. It is my prayer that the words have spoken to you at some point and you have grown in your knowledge of the Lord.

For this last chapter I simply want to encourage you to follow after what God has for you. He knows what is best for you. No matter what it costs, it will be well worth the trip to follow after Christ.

You may have studied this book and said that there is no way that you can ever be a woman of honor and influence because it is just too much to do. It is overwhelming at times when you try to look at everything that God requires of you. However, instead of looking at everything that you need to do or not do, look to Jesus. If you will pattern your life after His, then you will be on the right path. If you will simply commit to honoring God in everything that you do, you will find yourself being the woman God wants you to be.

Each of us must remember that we are influencing those around us every day. The question is whether we are a good or bad influence. Jesus said in Matthew 5:13-16 that we are to influence others as salt and light. Salt enhances the flavor of

A Work in Progress

foods and is used as a preservative. Are you enhancing the lives of those around you in a positive way? Are you helping to preserve their lives? You can do this by honoring God with your life. Light dispels darkness. Are you allowing your light to shine so as to dispel the darkness of this world around you? Your light is to shine brightly so that God may be glorified and honored.

I challenge you to be the woman that God wants you to be. Put away the things from your life that do not honor Him. *"Finally, brethren, whatsoever things are true, whatsoever things are honest, whatsoever things are just, whatsoever things are pure, whatsoever things are lovely, whatsoever things are of good report; if there be any virtue, and if there be any praise, think on these things"* (Philippians 4:8). Take time to study those characteristics on your own. Look them up in the dictionary, and run references in your Bible. Allow the Holy Spirit to speak to you and help you to *Become a Woman of Honor and Influence*.

God Bless!
Lisa Gothard
P. O. Box 611
Splendora, TX 77372

Honoring God and Influencing Others

Chapter 10
Q & A
for Thought

Am I honoring God and influencing others with my life right now?

What changes do I need to make in order to honor God and influence others?

What do I need to continue doing as I honor God and influence others?

A Work in Progress